50 Premium Feast Dishes for Home

By: Kelly Johnson

Table of Contents

- Beef Wellington
- Lobster Thermidor
- Coq au Vin
- Duck à l'Orange
- Rack of Lamb with Herb Crust
- Prime Rib Roast
- Truffle Risotto
- Filet Mignon with Red Wine Reduction
- Seafood Paella
- Osso Buco
- Bouillabaisse
- Porchetta
- Chateaubriand with Béarnaise Sauce
- Whole Roast Suckling Pig
- Bœuf Bourguignon
- Moroccan Lamb Tagine
- Whole Roast Turkey with Stuffing
- Surf and Turf (Steak & Lobster)
- Roasted Peking Duck
- Foie Gras with Fig Compote
- Honey-Glazed Ham
- Salmon en Croûte
- King Crab Legs with Garlic Butter
- Chicken Cordon Bleu
- Stuffed Leg of Lamb
- Seafood Tower with Oysters and Caviar
- Truffle Butter Roast Chicken
- Korean BBQ Short Ribs (Galbi)
- Whole Grilled Branzino
- Pasta with Lobster and Cognac Cream Sauce
- Braised Veal Shanks
- Herb-Crusted Venison Loin
- French Onion Soup Gratinée
- Crab-Stuffed Mushrooms
- Wild Mushroom and Parmesan Risotto

- Italian Porcini Mushroom Lasagna
- Pâté en Croûte
- Wagyu Beef Burgers with Truffle Aioli
- Grilled Tomahawk Steak
- Saffron-Infused Bouillabaisse
- Champagne-Poached Lobster Tail
- Prosciutto-Wrapped Asparagus
- Black Cod Miso (Nobu-Style)
- Grilled Lamb Chops with Mint Pesto
- Handmade Ricotta Gnocchi with Brown Butter Sage
- Roast Quail with Pomegranate Glaze
- Butter-Basted Scallops with Lemon Zest
- Slow-Cooked Barbecue Brisket
- Pan-Seared Halibut with Beurre Blanc
- Pistachio-Crusted Rack of Veal

Beef Wellington

A perfectly cooked beef tenderloin wrapped in puff pastry with mushroom duxelles and prosciutto.

Ingredients:

- 2 lb beef tenderloin
- 1 tbsp olive oil
- 2 tbsp Dijon mustard
- 8 oz mushrooms, finely chopped
- 2 tbsp butter
- 4 slices prosciutto
- 1 sheet puff pastry
- 1 egg yolk + 1 tbsp water (egg wash)

Instructions:

1. Sear the beef in olive oil until browned on all sides. Let cool and brush with Dijon mustard.
2. Cook mushrooms in butter until moisture evaporates. Let cool.
3. Lay prosciutto on plastic wrap, spread mushroom mixture on top, and wrap around the beef.
4. Roll in puff pastry, seal edges, and brush with egg wash.
5. Bake at 400°F (200°C) for 30-35 minutes. Let rest before slicing.

Lobster Thermidor

A rich, creamy French dish of lobster meat in a brandy-mustard sauce, baked in the shell.

Ingredients:

- 2 lobsters (1.5 lb each)
- 2 tbsp butter
- 2 tbsp flour
- 1 cup milk
- ¼ cup heavy cream
- ¼ cup brandy
- 1 tbsp Dijon mustard
- ½ cup grated Gruyère cheese
- Salt and pepper

Instructions:

1. Boil lobsters for 6 minutes, cool, and remove meat. Save shells for serving.
2. Make a roux with butter and flour, then whisk in milk, cream, and brandy.
3. Add mustard, lobster meat, and Gruyère. Stir and season.
4. Spoon mixture into lobster shells, top with more cheese, and broil until golden.

Coq au Vin

A slow-cooked French dish featuring chicken braised in red wine with mushrooms and bacon.

Ingredients:

- 1 whole chicken, cut into pieces
- 4 slices bacon, chopped
- 2 tbsp butter
- 1 onion, chopped
- 2 cloves garlic, minced
- 2 cups red wine
- 1 cup chicken broth
- 1 tbsp tomato paste
- 8 oz mushrooms, sliced
- Salt and pepper

Instructions:

1. Cook bacon until crispy, then remove. Brown chicken in the bacon fat.
2. Sauté onions and garlic, then add wine, broth, and tomato paste.
3. Return chicken and bacon to the pot, cover, and simmer for 1.5 hours.
4. Add mushrooms in the last 20 minutes. Serve warm.

Duck à l'Orange

A French classic with crispy duck and a sweet, tangy orange sauce.

Ingredients:

- 1 whole duck (4-5 lbs)
- Salt and pepper
- 1 cup orange juice
- ½ cup chicken stock
- ¼ cup white wine vinegar
- 2 tbsp sugar
- 1 tbsp Grand Marnier (optional)
- 1 orange, zested and sliced

Instructions:

1. Season duck and roast at 375°F (190°C) for 2 hours, basting occasionally.
2. Simmer vinegar and sugar until caramelized, then add juice, stock, and zest. Reduce.
3. Add Grand Marnier, then strain the sauce. Serve over duck.

Rack of Lamb with Herb Crust

A tender, flavorful lamb dish with a crispy herb crust.

Ingredients:

- 1 rack of lamb (8 ribs)
- 2 tbsp olive oil
- 2 tbsp Dijon mustard
- ½ cup breadcrumbs
- 2 tbsp parsley, chopped
- 2 tbsp rosemary, chopped
- Salt and pepper

Instructions:

1. Sear lamb in olive oil. Brush with Dijon mustard.
2. Mix breadcrumbs, herbs, salt, and pepper. Press onto lamb.
3. Roast at 400°F (200°C) for 20-25 minutes. Let rest before slicing.

Prime Rib Roast

A showstopping, juicy cut of beef with a crisp outer crust.

Ingredients:

- 1 prime rib roast (5-6 lbs)
- 3 tbsp olive oil
- 2 tbsp salt
- 2 tbsp black pepper
- 1 tbsp garlic powder
- 1 tbsp rosemary, chopped

Instructions:

1. Rub roast with oil and seasonings.
2. Roast at 450°F (230°C) for 20 minutes, then reduce to 325°F (165°C).
3. Cook until internal temp reaches 125°F (52°C) for medium-rare. Rest before slicing.

Truffle Risotto

A creamy, indulgent risotto infused with earthy truffle flavor.

Ingredients:

- 1 cup Arborio rice
- 4 cups chicken stock
- ½ cup white wine
- 1 small onion, chopped
- 2 tbsp butter
- ¼ cup Parmesan cheese
- 1 tbsp truffle oil
- Salt and pepper

Instructions:

1. Sauté onions in butter. Add rice and cook for 1 minute.
2. Deglaze with wine. Gradually add stock, stirring until absorbed.
3. Stir in Parmesan, truffle oil, and season to taste.

Filet Mignon with Red Wine Reduction

A tender steak with a luxurious red wine sauce.

Ingredients:

- 2 filet mignon steaks
- 1 tbsp olive oil
- 2 tbsp butter
- ½ cup red wine
- ¼ cup beef broth
- 1 shallot, minced
- 1 tsp fresh thyme

Instructions:

1. Sear steaks in oil for 3-4 minutes per side. Remove and rest.
2. Sauté shallots in butter, add wine and broth, and reduce.
3. Stir in thyme and butter. Serve sauce over steaks.

Seafood Paella

A vibrant Spanish rice dish with seafood, saffron, and vegetables.

Ingredients:

- 2 cups Arborio rice
- 4 cups seafood broth
- 1 tsp saffron
- 1 onion, chopped
- 1 red bell pepper, sliced
- 1 tomato, diced
- 1 cup shrimp
- 1 cup mussels
- 1 cup calamari
- 2 tbsp olive oil

Instructions:

1. Sauté onion, pepper, and tomato in oil. Add rice and saffron.
2. Pour in broth, simmer for 10 minutes.
3. Add seafood and cook until tender. Serve hot.

Osso Buco

A Milanese dish of braised veal shanks in a flavorful sauce.

Ingredients:

- 4 veal shanks
- ½ cup flour
- 2 tbsp olive oil
- 1 onion, chopped
- 2 carrots, chopped
- 2 celery stalks, chopped
- 1 cup white wine
- 2 cups beef broth
- 1 can (14 oz) diced tomatoes
- 1 tbsp tomato paste
- 2 cloves garlic, minced
- 1 tbsp parsley

Instructions:

1. Dredge veal in flour and brown in oil. Remove.
2. Sauté onion, carrots, and celery. Add wine, broth, tomatoes, and paste.
3. Return veal, cover, and simmer for 2 hours. Garnish with parsley.

Bouillabaisse *(French Fisherman's Stew)*

A classic Provençal seafood stew with a rich saffron-infused broth.

Ingredients:

- 1 lb white fish fillets (cod, halibut)
- ½ lb mussels
- ½ lb shrimp
- 4 cups fish stock
- 1 cup dry white wine
- 2 tbsp olive oil
- 1 onion, chopped
- 2 tomatoes, diced
- 2 cloves garlic, minced
- 1 tsp saffron
- ½ tsp cayenne pepper
- 1 bay leaf
- Salt and pepper

Instructions:

1. Sauté onion, garlic, and tomatoes in olive oil. Add saffron and cayenne.
2. Pour in stock and wine, then simmer for 15 minutes.
3. Add fish, shrimp, and mussels. Cook until seafood is tender.
4. Serve with crusty bread and rouille sauce.

Porchetta *(Italian Herb-Roasted Pork Belly)*

A crispy-skinned, herb-stuffed Italian pork roast.

Ingredients:

- 5 lb pork belly, skin on
- 3 cloves garlic, minced
- 2 tbsp rosemary, chopped
- 2 tbsp fennel seeds, crushed
- 1 tbsp black pepper
- 2 tbsp olive oil
- Salt

Instructions:

1. Score pork skin. Rub with garlic, herbs, fennel, and olive oil.
2. Roll tightly and tie with butcher's twine.
3. Roast at 325°F (160°C) for 4 hours, then crisp skin at 450°F (230°C) for 30 minutes.

Chateaubriand with Béarnaise Sauce *(Classic French Steak for Two)*

A thick-cut beef tenderloin, served with a rich, buttery Béarnaise sauce.

Ingredients:

- 1 lb beef tenderloin
- 2 tbsp butter
- Salt and pepper

Béarnaise Sauce:

- 2 tbsp white wine vinegar
- 1 shallot, minced
- 1 tsp tarragon
- 2 egg yolks
- ½ cup melted butter

Instructions:

1. Sear tenderloin in butter, then roast at 400°F (200°C) for 15 minutes.
2. For the sauce, simmer vinegar, shallot, and tarragon, then whisk with egg yolks and melted butter.
3. Slice steak and serve with sauce.

Whole Roast Suckling Pig *(Crispy and Juicy Celebration Dish)*

A festive centerpiece with crispy skin and tender meat.

Ingredients:

- 1 whole suckling pig (8-12 lbs)
- ¼ cup olive oil
- 2 tbsp salt
- 1 tbsp black pepper
- 2 tbsp garlic powder

Instructions:

1. Preheat oven to 325°F (160°C).
2. Rub pig with oil, salt, and seasonings.
3. Roast for 4-5 hours, basting frequently.
4. Crisp skin at 450°F (230°C) for the last 20 minutes.

Bœuf Bourguignon *(French Red Wine Beef Stew)*

A rich beef stew braised in red wine with mushrooms, carrots, and pearl onions.

Ingredients:

- 2 lbs beef chuck, cubed
- ½ lb bacon, chopped
- 2 cups red wine
- 2 cups beef broth
- 1 onion, chopped
- 2 carrots, sliced
- 8 oz mushrooms, quartered
- 2 tbsp tomato paste
- 2 cloves garlic, minced
- 1 bay leaf

Instructions:

1. Sear beef and bacon, then remove.
2. Sauté onions, carrots, and mushrooms.
3. Add tomato paste, garlic, and bay leaf, then return beef.
4. Pour in wine and broth. Simmer for 2.5 hours.

Moroccan Lamb Tagine *(Slow-Cooked Spiced Lamb Stew)*

A fragrant North African dish with tender lamb, apricots, and warming spices.

Ingredients:

- 2 lbs lamb shoulder, cubed
- 1 onion, chopped
- 2 cloves garlic, minced
- 1 tsp cinnamon
- 1 tsp cumin
- ½ tsp ginger
- ½ cup dried apricots
- 2 cups beef broth

Instructions:

1. Brown lamb and remove.
2. Sauté onions and garlic, add spices.
3. Return lamb, add apricots and broth.
4. Simmer for 2 hours. Serve with couscous.

Whole Roast Turkey with Stuffing *(Classic Holiday Turkey)*

A juicy roasted turkey with a flavorful stuffing.

Ingredients:

- 12 lb turkey
- ¼ cup butter, melted
- Salt and pepper

Stuffing:

- 4 cups bread cubes
- 1 onion, chopped
- 2 celery stalks, chopped
- 1 tbsp sage
- 1 cup chicken broth

Instructions:

1. Stuff turkey with the stuffing mixture.
2. Brush turkey with butter, season, and roast at 325°F (160°C) for 4 hours.

Surf and Turf (Steak & Lobster) *(The Ultimate Indulgence)*

A luxurious pairing of filet mignon and butter-poached lobster.

Ingredients:

- 2 filet mignon steaks
- 2 lobster tails
- 2 tbsp butter

Instructions:

1. Sear steaks to desired doneness.
2. Broil lobster tails with butter until cooked.
3. Serve together with garlic butter.

Roasted Peking Duck *(Crispy-Skinned Chinese Delicacy)*

A famous Beijing dish with crispy skin and tender meat.

Ingredients:

- 1 whole duck
- 2 tbsp honey
- 1 tbsp soy sauce
- 1 tsp five-spice powder

Instructions:

1. Hang duck in a cool place for 24 hours.
2. Brush with honey-soy glaze.
3. Roast at 375°F (190°C) for 1.5 hours.
4. Serve with pancakes and hoisin sauce.

Foie Gras with Fig Compote *(French Luxury Appetizer)*

Rich foie gras paired with sweet fig compote.

Ingredients:

- 4 foie gras slices
- Salt and pepper
- 1 cup figs, chopped
- ¼ cup red wine
- 1 tbsp honey

Instructions:

1. Sear foie gras for 1 minute per side.
2. Simmer figs with wine and honey.
3. Serve foie gras with compote.

Honey-Glazed Ham *(Sweet & Savory Holiday Classic)*

A succulent ham coated in a sweet honey glaze.

Ingredients:

- 1 whole ham (8 lbs)
- ½ cup honey
- ¼ cup brown sugar
- 2 tbsp Dijon mustard
- 1 tsp cloves

Instructions:

1. Score ham and bake at 325°F (160°C) for 2 hours.
2. Mix honey, sugar, and mustard.
3. Glaze ham and bake another 30 minutes.

Salmon en Croûte *(Salmon Wrapped in Puff Pastry)*

A golden, flaky pastry encasing tender salmon with a flavorful filling.

Ingredients:

- 2 salmon fillets (6 oz each)
- 1 sheet puff pastry
- 2 tbsp Dijon mustard
- ½ cup spinach, sautéed
- ¼ cup cream cheese
- 1 egg, beaten (for egg wash)
- Salt and pepper

Instructions:

1. Spread mustard on salmon. Mix spinach with cream cheese and spread on top.
2. Wrap in puff pastry and brush with egg wash.
3. Bake at 400°F (200°C) for 20-25 minutes.

King Crab Legs with Garlic Butter *(Sweet, Succulent Crab Legs)*

Steamed or grilled king crab legs served with rich garlic butter.

Ingredients:

- 2 lbs king crab legs
- ½ cup butter, melted
- 3 cloves garlic, minced
- 1 tbsp lemon juice
- 1 tsp paprika

Instructions:

1. Steam crab legs for 5 minutes.
2. Mix melted butter with garlic, lemon, and paprika.
3. Serve with warm crab legs.

Chicken Cordon Bleu *(Crispy Chicken Stuffed with Ham and Cheese)*

A breaded chicken breast filled with ham and Swiss cheese.

Ingredients:

- 2 chicken breasts, pounded thin
- 2 slices ham
- 2 slices Swiss cheese
- ½ cup flour
- 1 egg, beaten
- ½ cup breadcrumbs

Instructions:

1. Lay ham and cheese on chicken, roll up, and secure with toothpicks.
2. Dredge in flour, dip in egg, and coat in breadcrumbs.
3. Bake at 375°F (190°C) for 25 minutes.

Stuffed Leg of Lamb *(Tender Roast with a Flavorful Filling)*

A juicy, herb-stuffed lamb roast with Mediterranean flavors.

Ingredients:

- 1 boneless leg of lamb (4 lbs)
- 2 cloves garlic, minced
- 1 cup spinach
- ½ cup feta cheese
- 1 tbsp rosemary, chopped
- 1 tbsp olive oil

Instructions:

1. Butterfly lamb and spread with garlic, spinach, feta, and rosemary.
2. Roll and tie with butcher's twine.
3. Roast at 350°F (175°C) for 1.5 hours.

Seafood Tower with Oysters and Caviar *(Luxury Seafood Platter)*

A stunning display of fresh seafood, oysters, shrimp, and caviar.

Ingredients:

- 12 oysters, shucked
- 8 shrimp, cooked
- 4 oz lump crab meat
- 2 oz caviar
- Lemon wedges
- Cocktail sauce

Instructions:

1. Arrange oysters, shrimp, and crab on a tiered platter.
2. Serve with lemon wedges and cocktail sauce.
3. Top with caviar and enjoy chilled.

Truffle Butter Roast Chicken *(Crispy, Juicy Chicken with Truffle Aroma)*

A whole roasted chicken infused with truffle butter.

Ingredients:

- 1 whole chicken (4-5 lbs)
- 3 tbsp truffle butter
- 2 cloves garlic, minced
- 1 tbsp rosemary

Instructions:

1. Rub chicken with truffle butter, garlic, and rosemary.
2. Roast at 375°F (190°C) for 1 hour 15 minutes.

Korean BBQ Short Ribs (Galbi) *(Sweet and Savory Grilled Beef Ribs)*

Tender, marinated beef short ribs grilled to perfection.

Ingredients:

- 2 lbs beef short ribs (flanken cut)
- ¼ cup soy sauce
- 2 tbsp brown sugar
- 1 tbsp sesame oil
- 2 cloves garlic, minced
- 1 tsp grated ginger

Instructions:

1. Marinate ribs for at least 4 hours.
2. Grill over high heat for 3-4 minutes per side.

Whole Grilled Branzino *(Mediterranean-Style Grilled Fish)*

A whole branzino grilled with fresh herbs and citrus.

Ingredients:

- 1 whole branzino, cleaned
- 2 tbsp olive oil
- 1 lemon, sliced
- 2 cloves garlic, minced
- 1 tbsp fresh thyme

Instructions:

1. Stuff fish with lemon, garlic, and thyme.
2. Brush with olive oil and grill for 5 minutes per side.

Pasta with Lobster and Cognac Cream Sauce *(Rich and Indulgent Pasta Dish)*

Lobster tossed in a luxurious cognac cream sauce.

Ingredients:

- 1 lb lobster tail meat
- ½ lb pasta
- ½ cup heavy cream
- ¼ cup cognac
- 2 tbsp butter
- 2 cloves garlic, minced

Instructions:

1. Sauté garlic in butter, then add lobster and cognac.
2. Stir in cream and simmer. Toss with pasta.

Braised Veal Shanks (Osso Buco) *(Italian Slow-Braised Veal)*

Fall-off-the-bone veal shanks braised in wine and broth.

Ingredients:

- 2 veal shanks
- ½ cup white wine
- 2 cups beef broth
- 1 onion, chopped
- 2 cloves garlic, minced
- 1 tsp thyme

Instructions:

1. Sear veal shanks, then remove.
2. Sauté onions and garlic, then add shanks back.
3. Pour in wine and broth. Simmer for 2 hours.

Herb-Crusted Venison Loin *(Tender, Flavorful Wild Game Dish)*

A lean venison loin with a crisp herb crust.

Ingredients:

- 1 venison loin (1 lb)
- 2 tbsp Dijon mustard
- ½ cup breadcrumbs
- 1 tbsp rosemary
- 1 tbsp thyme

Instructions:

1. Coat venison in mustard, then press in herbs and breadcrumbs.
2. Roast at 375°F (190°C) for 20 minutes.

French Onion Soup Gratinée *(Rich, caramelized onion soup with melted cheese)*

A comforting and flavorful classic French soup.

Ingredients:

- 4 large onions, thinly sliced
- 4 tbsp butter
- 1 tbsp olive oil
- 4 cups beef broth
- 1 cup white wine
- 1 tsp thyme
- 1 baguette, sliced
- 1½ cups Gruyère cheese, grated

Instructions:

1. Sauté onions in butter and oil until caramelized.
2. Add wine, broth, and thyme. Simmer for 30 minutes.
3. Pour into bowls, top with toasted baguette slices and cheese.
4. Broil until cheese is melted and golden.

Crab-Stuffed Mushrooms *(Savory mushrooms filled with a rich crab mixture)*

A luxurious appetizer with a creamy seafood filling.

Ingredients:

- 12 large mushrooms, stems removed
- ½ cup crab meat
- ¼ cup cream cheese
- 1 tbsp mayonnaise
- 1 tbsp Parmesan cheese
- 1 garlic clove, minced

Instructions:

1. Mix crab, cream cheese, mayo, Parmesan, and garlic.
2. Stuff mushrooms and bake at 375°F (190°C) for 15 minutes.

Wild Mushroom and Parmesan Risotto *(Creamy, earthy risotto with Parmesan)*

A rich Italian dish made with arborio rice and wild mushrooms.

Ingredients:

- 1½ cups arborio rice
- 4 cups chicken broth
- 1 cup wild mushrooms, sliced
- ½ cup white wine
- ½ cup Parmesan cheese
- 2 tbsp butter

Instructions:

1. Sauté mushrooms, then add rice and toast slightly.
2. Add wine, then broth gradually while stirring.
3. Stir in butter and Parmesan before serving.

Italian Porcini Mushroom Lasagna *(Layers of pasta, creamy sauce, and porcini mushrooms)*

A decadent, cheesy lasagna with deep umami flavors.

Ingredients:

- 12 lasagna sheets
- 1 cup dried porcini mushrooms, rehydrated
- 2 cups béchamel sauce
- 1 cup ricotta cheese
- ½ cup Parmesan cheese
- ½ cup mozzarella cheese

Instructions:

1. Layer pasta, mushrooms, ricotta, béchamel, and cheese.
2. Repeat layers and bake at 375°F (190°C) for 30 minutes.

Pâté en Croûte *(French pâté baked in a flaky crust)*

A sophisticated terrine with a buttery pastry shell.

Ingredients:

- 1 sheet puff pastry
- 1 lb pork and veal pâté
- 1 egg, beaten (for egg wash)

Instructions:

1. Wrap pâté in puff pastry, brush with egg wash.
2. Bake at 375°F (190°C) for 30 minutes.

Wagyu Beef Burgers with Truffle Aioli *(Juicy Wagyu beef with a luxurious aioli)*

A gourmet burger with rich, high-quality beef.

Ingredients:

- 2 Wagyu beef patties
- 2 brioche buns
- 2 tbsp truffle aioli
- 2 slices aged cheddar
- 1 tbsp butter

Instructions:

1. Grill Wagyu patties to preferred doneness.
2. Toast buns with butter.
3. Assemble with cheese and aioli.

Grilled Tomahawk Steak *(Massive, flavorful steak with a perfect sear)*

A show-stopping steak with a crispy crust.

Ingredients:

- 1 tomahawk steak (2 lbs)
- 2 tbsp olive oil
- 1 tbsp sea salt
- 1 tbsp cracked black pepper

Instructions:

1. Season steak, sear on high heat, then grill until desired doneness.
2. Rest for 10 minutes before slicing.

Saffron-Infused Bouillabaisse *(French seafood stew with saffron broth)*

A luxurious Provençal fish stew.

Ingredients:

- 2 cups fish stock
- ½ cup white wine
- 1 pinch saffron
- 1 lb mixed seafood (shrimp, mussels, white fish)
- 2 tomatoes, diced
- 1 onion, chopped

Instructions:

1. Sauté onions and tomatoes, add wine and stock.
2. Simmer with saffron, add seafood, and cook for 5 minutes.

Champagne-Poached Lobster Tail *(Tender lobster infused with champagne)*

A delicate, elegant seafood dish.

Ingredients:

- 2 lobster tails
- 1 cup champagne
- 2 tbsp butter
- 1 tsp chives

Instructions:

1. Poach lobster in champagne for 5 minutes.
2. Drizzle with butter and garnish with chives.

Prosciutto-Wrapped Asparagus *(Crispy, savory asparagus wrapped in prosciutto)*

A simple yet delicious appetizer.

Ingredients:

- 12 asparagus spears
- 6 slices prosciutto
- 1 tbsp olive oil

Instructions:

1. Wrap asparagus in prosciutto.
2. Bake at 375°F (190°C) for 10 minutes.

Black Cod Miso (Nobu-Style) *(Silky, miso-marinated black cod)*

A classic Japanese dish with a rich, umami-packed glaze.

Ingredients:

- 2 black cod fillets
- ¼ cup white miso paste
- 3 tbsp mirin
- 2 tbsp sake
- 2 tbsp sugar

Instructions:

1. Mix miso, mirin, sake, and sugar. Marinate cod for 24 hours.
2. Broil or grill for 8–10 minutes until golden.

Grilled Lamb Chops with Mint Pesto *(Juicy lamb chops with a fresh, herby sauce)*

A perfect balance of rich meat and refreshing mint.

Ingredients:

- 8 lamb chops
- 2 tbsp olive oil
- 1 tsp salt
- ½ tsp black pepper
- 1 cup fresh mint leaves
- ½ cup parsley
- 2 tbsp lemon juice
- ¼ cup olive oil
- ¼ cup grated Parmesan

Instructions:

1. Season lamb, grill 4 minutes per side.
2. Blend mint, parsley, lemon juice, olive oil, and Parmesan for pesto.
3. Serve with grilled lamb.

Handmade Ricotta Gnocchi with Brown Butter Sage *(Pillowy gnocchi in a nutty butter sauce)*

A delicate and comforting Italian dish.

Ingredients:

- 1 cup ricotta cheese
- ½ cup flour
- 1 egg yolk
- ¼ cup Parmesan cheese
- 4 tbsp butter
- 6 sage leaves

Instructions:

1. Mix ricotta, flour, egg yolk, and Parmesan. Roll and cut into gnocchi.
2. Boil until they float.
3. Sauté in brown butter with sage.

Roast Quail with Pomegranate Glaze *(Tender quail with a sweet-tart glaze)*

A gourmet dish with a stunning presentation.

Ingredients:

- 4 whole quails
- 2 tbsp olive oil
- ½ tsp salt
- ½ cup pomegranate juice
- 2 tbsp honey
- 1 tbsp balsamic vinegar

Instructions:

1. Roast quails at 400°F (200°C) for 20 minutes.
2. Reduce pomegranate juice, honey, and vinegar into a glaze.
3. Brush quail with glaze before serving.

Butter-Basted Scallops with Lemon Zest *(Perfectly seared scallops with rich butter sauce)*

A delicate seafood dish with citrus brightness.

Ingredients:

- 8 large sea scallops
- 2 tbsp butter
- 1 tbsp olive oil
- ½ tsp salt
- 1 tsp lemon zest

Instructions:

1. Sear scallops in oil for 2 minutes per side.
2. Add butter and lemon zest, spoon over scallops for 1 minute.

Slow-Cooked Barbecue Brisket *(Smoky, fall-apart tender brisket)*

A rich and flavorful BBQ staple.

Ingredients:

- 3 lb beef brisket
- 2 tbsp paprika
- 1 tbsp garlic powder
- 1 tbsp brown sugar
- 1 cup barbecue sauce

Instructions:

1. Rub brisket with spices, slow cook at 275°F (135°C) for 6 hours.
2. Brush with BBQ sauce and broil for 5 minutes.

Pan-Seared Halibut with Beurre Blanc *(Crispy halibut with a luscious butter sauce)*

A refined seafood dish with French elegance.

Ingredients:

- 2 halibut fillets
- 2 tbsp butter
- ½ cup white wine
- 1 shallot, minced
- ½ cup heavy cream

Instructions:

1. Sear halibut 3 minutes per side.
2. Simmer shallots in wine, add cream and butter for sauce.
3. Serve sauce over halibut.

Pistachio-Crusted Rack of Veal *(Tender veal with a crunchy nut crust)*

A luxurious main course with depth of flavor.

Ingredients:

- 1 rack of veal
- ½ cup pistachios, finely chopped
- 2 tbsp Dijon mustard
- 1 tbsp olive oil

Instructions:

1. Brush veal with mustard, coat with pistachios.
2. Roast at 375°F (190°C) for 25 minutes.

www.ingramcontent.com/pod-product-compliance
Lightning Source LLC
LaVergne TN
LVHW081459060526
838201LV00056BA/2840